The Battle of Spioenkop

23-24 January 1900

Gilbert Torlage

RAVAN PRESS

The Battle Book Series

- The Battle of Talana
- The Battle of Elandslaagte
- The Battle of Colenso
- The Battle of Spioenkop
- The Battle of Vaalkrans
- The Battle of the Thukela Heights
- The Siege of Ladysmith

First published in 1999

Ravan Press
P O Box 145, Randburg 2125

© Gilbert Torlage

ISBN: 0 86975 516 1

DTP and design by: Heather Brooksbank, Resolution

Cover Design: David Selfe, Dark Horse Design

Cartography: Toni Bodington & Olive Anderson
   Cartographic Unit, University of Natal (Pietermaritzburg)

Photographs and sketches from: the KwaZulu-Natal Provincial
   Museum Service Collection

Lithographic repro by: 3 White Dogs

Contents

Anglo-Boer War Sites

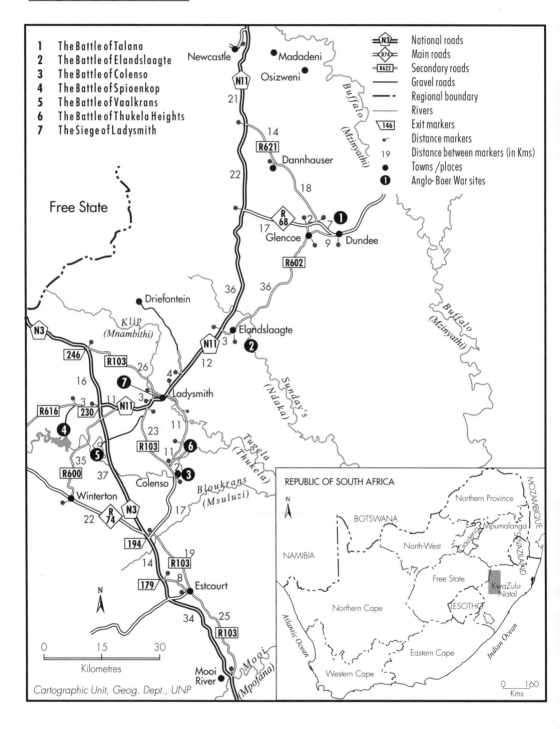

1 The Battle of Talana
2 The Battle of Elandslaagte
3 The Battle of Colenso
4 The Battle of Spioenkop
5 The Battle of Vaalkrans
6 The Battle of Thukela Heights
7 The Siege of Ladysmith

National roads
Main roads
Secondary roads
Gravel roads
Regional boundary
Rivers
Exit markers
Distance markers
Distance between markers (in Kms)
Towns /places
Anglo-Boer War sites

Free State

Newcastle
Madadeni
Osizweni
Dannhauser
Glencoe
Dundee
Driefontein
Elandslaagte
Ladysmith
Winterton
Colenso
Estcourt
Mooi River

Buffalo (Mzinyathi)
Klip (Mnambithi)
Sunday's (Ndaka)
Tugela (Thukela)
Bloukrans (Msuluzi)
Mooi (Mpofana)

0   15   30
Kilometres

Cartographic Unit, Geog. Dept., UNP

REPUBLIC OF SOUTH AFRICA

Northern Province
BOTSWANA
Mpumalanga
North-West
Gauteng
MOZAMBIQUE
SWAZILAND
NAMIBIA
Free State
KwaZulu-Natal
LESOTHO
Northern Cape
Atlantic Ocean
Eastern Cape
Western Cape
Indian Ocean

0   160
Kms

Preface

This Battle Book series has been written to make information, photographs and maps of the most significant Anglo-Boer War sites in KwaZulu-Natal more readily available.

The books are not exhaustive studies of the various sites but rather field guides, designed to assist the reader in interpreting the terrain and understanding the events.

Although the Battle Books form a series, each book has been fully contextualised and can be followed on its own.

Contributors to this series share a long-term interest in the Anglo-Boer War and have each made their own unique contribution to the historiography and understanding of the conflict. With the assistance of an editorial committee, every effort has been made to maintain balance and accuracy.

A slightly flexible approach has been adopted to the spelling of names. As a general rule, the most recent spelling utilised on the state's Survey and Mapping 1:50 000 maps has been adopted. Thus for instance Laing's Nek becomes Lang's Nek. Where the name used to describe a topographical feature differs significantly from that in the historical literature to that appearing on the map, then the one used in the books and documents is adopted. The spelling of the river Thukela (Tugela) presents a slight problem. On the maps it is spelt as given in the brackets. However, in most current academic historical literature the former form has been adopted, which spelling has been followed in this series of books.

At 17:00 on 11 October 1899 the ultimatum handed by the South African Republic's Secretary of State, FW Reitz, to the British Resident in Pretoria, expired. The two Boer republics were now formally at war with Great Britain. The first Boers, commanded by Commandant-General PJ Joubert, soon entered the British colony of Natal, determined to overcome the large concentration of troops stationed at Dundee and Ladysmith threatening their sovereignty. After quick victories at Dundee (20 October), Nicholson's Nek (30 October) and a defeat at Elandslaagte (21 October), the Boers besieged Ladysmith early in November 1899. Trapped in the town were 13 000 troops, their 2 500 servants and 5 400 civilians.

In early November the Boers attempted to force the troops trapped in Ladysmith to capitulate, but failed. A few days later a commando numbering approximately 2 000 burghers made a foray south into Natal, reaching as far as Mooi River; however, as they encountered a growing number of British troops advancing from the south, the Boers decided to withdraw to defensive positions just north of the Thukela (Tugela) River at Colenso. They dug in here and were reinforced until they numbered 4 500. These Boers, commanded by the young, dynamic but inexperienced General Louis Botha, were determined to prevent a British force from relieving Ladysmith.

Meanwhile, General Sir Redvers Buller VC, with a force of 47 000 men had been despatched from Britain to command the British forces engaged in the South African war. Buller, the great hero and experienced general, upon whom all Britain pinned their hopes to bring the war to a speedy and successful end, was given a rousing farewell by the British public. On his arrival at Cape Town he was

met by the almost unbelievable news that the Boers had besieged Ladysmith, Mafeking (Mafikeng) and Kimberley and that they were invading the north-eastern Cape.

To counter this situation Buller split his force of 47 000 men into three. One force was to relieve Kimberley and Mafeking, another to halt the Boer advance into the north-eastern Cape, while the third and largest, under Buller's personal command, was to land in Durban and relieve Ladysmith. It was part of this force that the Boer commando of 2 000 burghers had encountered during their foray south into Natal.

On 15 December 1899, Buller, supported by 19 400 men, attempted to force his way through Botha's defensive line at Colenso. In a short, but sharp engagement, the British force was repulsed, losing over a thousand men and ten field guns. Botha's losses were a mere 38 men. Buller's reputation, pride and, more seriously, his confidence, had suffered a stunning blow. His shaken confidence is illustrated by a telegram he sent to the Secretary for War in which he stated, "My failure today raises a serious question. I do not think I am now strong enough to relieve White." To compound Buller's personal agony, he was replaced by Field Marshal Lord Roberts VC as commander-in-chief, and was henceforth only in command of the Natal Field Force. Buller and Roberts came from opposing factions within the British army and were not well disposed to one another.

For a while after the Colenso reverse, Buller remained on the defensive; however, the arrival of the 5th Division under Lieutenant-General Sir Charles Warren as reinforcements and the Boer attempt on 6 January to smash the defensive perimeter around Ladysmith, prompted him to make another effort to relieve the town.

Early on 10 January Buller's forces encamped at Chievely and Frere set off, headed towards the upper Thukela, where he hoped to cross

General Buller's men departing from their Frere camp on 10 January 1900. In the foreground is the 28th Battery Royal Field Artillery.

the river and make his way across the plains to Ladysmith. The Boers already had approximately 1 000 men and one gun on the upper Thukela. When Botha noticed the British troop movements, he sent a few hundred men to reinforce the upper Thukela position and also requested Joubert to let him have further reinforcements from the men surrounding Ladysmith. By the time the British forces arrived near Potgieter's Drift they found the heights across the river entrenched and occupied.

Buller concluded that crossing via Potgieter's Drift would be too costly. He therefore decided that he would hold Mount Alice and Potgieter's Drift with approximately 9 000 men and some guns, while Warren, with 15 000 men and 36 guns, was ordered to cross the Thukela approximately five kilometres upstream at Trichardt's Drift and then swing around the high ground west of Spioenkop. Once around the high ground he was to move in behind the Boers on Brakfontein opposite Buller, making their position untenable. Once they retired, Buller would cross the river, join Warren and march to the relief of Ladysmith. Intelligence sources maintained Warren would have to contend with only approximately 400 Boers.

Boer trenches on the Brakfontein heights. In the background are the Twin Peaks. By the time Buller's force arrived at Mt Alice the Boers were entrenched on the high ground opposite them.

Warren, second in command to Buller, was a curious choice to lead this potentially hazardous undertaking. Before coming to South Africa he had retired from active service. Furthermore his experience of commanding men in times of war was limited. Never had Warren seen or commanded a force as large as the one he was to lead. One is left with the impression that Buller's confidence had deserted him and consequently he was passing responsibility on to Warren, so that in the event of another defeat he would not be held personally responsible, especially in the light of the fact that the orders to Warren were rather vague and also stated, *"You will of course act as circumstances require..."*

iNtabamnyama failures

Late on 16 January the British move to outflank the Boers to the west began. Approximately 2 000 men and six guns crossed the Thukela at Potgieter's Drift and occupied the Maconochie Koppies. This convinced the Boers that an attempt was being made to breach their position at Brakfontein. They therefore reinforced this position, while leaving iNtabamnyama relatively unattended. Therefore, when Warren began crossing the Thukela early on 17 January at Trichardt's Drift, to where he had moved under cover of darkness, only 500 burghers defended iNtabamnyama. These burghers had no artillery and were not entrenched. Quick and decisive action at this stage would almost certainly have resulted in Botha's defence line being breached and Ladysmith relieved.

At the very time that Warren began crossing the Thukela the naval guns on and around Mount Alice opened a steady fire on the Boer

(COPYRIGHT) A STRIKING PICTURE - DRAWING ARTILLERY UP STEEP BANK OF THE TUGELA - BOER WAR

Lieutenant-General Warren's column crossing at Trichardt's Drift. It took many hours for the 15 000 men, 36 guns, 4 856 horses, supply wagons and oxen to negotiate the crossing.

positions opposite them, while infantry began demonstrations opposite Brakfontein as well as a little further downstream, creating the impression that this was where the main attack was to be made. For this reason a number of Boer officers were loath to send reinforcements to iNtabamnyama to counter the British advance over Trichardt's Drift.

Colonials (Natal Carbineers) under Colonel Lord Dundonald lying in ambush for a Boer patrol near Acton Homes, 18 January.

Consequently, other than firing a few rounds at Warren's men crossing the river, the Boers allowed his force to cross virtually unopposed. As the seriousness of the situation became clearer to the Boer officers and Botha in particular, reinforcements of men and guns were ordered to move west to iNtabamnyama, with instructions to dig themselves in. This flow of men to iNtabamnyama began on 17 January and continued until 22 January.

While Warren's infantry was still crossing on 18 January, his cavalry, under the command of Colonel Lord Dundonald, was instructed to scout the terrain to the north-west, towards Acton Homes. Near Acton Homes contact was made with approximately 160 burghers under command of Veld-Cornets Daniel Opperman and N Mentz. After a short, sharp skirmish the Boers were driven off and Dundonald took possession of strategic positions overlooking the Acton Homes – Ladysmith road. Here was a golden opportunity for Warren to turn the Boer line and enter the plain

British cavalry crossing at Trichardt's Drift got into difficulty and several were rescued by Trooper DG Sclanders. He received the Humane Society (silver class) award for his heroism.

behind them and indeed to push through to Ladysmith. He decided not to follow up, maintaining that that route was too long and dangerous, and angrily pointed out to Dundonald that he had exceeded his orders and that their task was not to reach Ladysmith, but link up with Buller and then to receive orders from him!

During 19 January Warren still made no attempt to attack the Boers, but moved about the Thukela valley rather ineffectually and only on 20 January did he finally attack. By this time the Boer force had grown to 1 800 men on iNtabamnyama,

Major-General Hart's men attacking on iNtabamnyama on 20 January. The Boers were well positioned and entrenched and easily repulsed the British.

supported by three guns and one quick firing Maxim-Nordenfeldt (Pom-Pom) gun. They were now well entrenched in expertly chosen positions. Before them they had fields of fire ranging between 600 and 1 000 metres. Furthermore, there was nowhere where the British could place their artillery either to effectively shell the Boer positions or indeed lend systematic supporting fire to attacking infantry on iNtabamnyama.

Consequently, when Warren's force finally attacked the Boer line on 20 and 21 January, it was repulsed relatively easily, with British losses numbering approximately 477 killed, wounded or missing as opposed to approximately 72 Boer burghers killed or wounded or missing. None the less the intensity of the British attack had caused the Boer line to waver in places, with many of the Johannesburg and Heidelberg burghers deserting. Botha knew that it was imperative that they hold their position. He was perfectly aware that if the much larger British force were to cross the high ground, there would be no other point at which they would be able to halt them. It would therefore be able to penetrate to Ladysmith and relieve the town. To check the sinking morale of his men, he moved up and down the defence lines, urging them to remain in their trenches and defend their positions. It may well be that his earlier success at Colenso had an important positive influence at this critical time.

For Warren to succeed it was necessary for him to change his tactics. He decided to resort to shelling the Boers for a few days in order to demoralise them. Considering the wavering Boer morale, this tactic may well have had the desired effect and indeed information received from the British in Ladysmith had made it known that a number of Boers had been seen leaving iNtabamnyama. On the morning of 22 January, however, Buller rode across to Warren's headquarters at Three Tree Hill to discuss tactics and immediately objected to the plan of shelling the Boers for a number of days, regarding the proposal as wasting time. He also objected to Warren's proposal that the men carry three to four days' supply in their haversacks, while the wagons returned to Mount Alice.

With that Warren is alleged to have said,

"It will be impossible to go by the Fair View road (over iNtabamnyama) without taking Spion Kop". To which Buller replied, "Of course you must take Spion Kop". Spioenkop was the highest point along the Boer defence line on the upper Thukela.

It appears that the decision to attack Spioenkop was given inadequate consideration. Was it really necessary to capture Spioenkop? What of significance could be achieved by its capture? Warren's knowledge of the geographic features of the summit and of the surrounding area was limited. He could see only one side of the hill. Much of the summit was hidden from him because it was higher than his own position. Nor did he know whether Spioenkop was defended or even defensible. What was quite evident was that the climb to the top would be a long and arduous one. The summit lies 400 metres above the river valley, from where Warren's men would have to advance.

After a series of setbacks the British senior officers appeared to be clutching at straws. Other than wishing to place a battery of mountain guns on the summit, Warren never stated why he wanted to capture Spioenkop. Boer artilley in the area would have outranged the mountain battery and negated it. The length and steepness of the spur to the Spioenkop summit would have made it extremely difficult, if not impossible, to take the mountain guns to the summit.

Warren now reorganised his force, dividing it into two parts. The left under Lieutenant-General F Clery and the right under Major-General JT Coke. From the right section a force was drawn to assault Spioenkop. Clery was given the discretion to create a diversion on iNtabamnyama during the attack on Spioenkop. On 23 January Warren rode out towards Spioenkop to view it from those angles available to him to find out as much about it as possible. However, as the Boers controlled it and the surrounding heights, it was impossible to gain a detailed and accurate picture of the entire hill. During 22 and 23 January the Boer and British forces kept up a steady, but rather ineffectual fire on one another.

Attack on Spioenkop

Warren and his senior officers decided to capture Spioenkop by surprise under the cover of darkness. A force of approximately 1 700 men of the 2nd Royal Lancaster Regiment, 2nd Lancashire Fusiliers, 1st South Lancashire Regiment, Thorneycroft's Mounted Infantry (a volunteer unit consisting mainly of 'Uitlanders') and a half company of 17th Royal Engineers, to be commanded by Major-General Woodgate, gathered at 19:00 on 23 January near Warren's camp. Their orders were to climb Spioenkop, surprise the Boers on the hill, drive them off and entrench themselves. Each man was to carry 150 rounds of ammunition, rifle, bayonet, rations and water. The Engineers would bring up entrenching equipment. Machine guns, a mountain battery (still on its way from Frere), additional ammunition and water were to be brought up later by mules.

The strategic importance of Spioenkop had not escaped the Boers. On 21 January Botha requested General Schalk Burger to inspect the summit with a view to placing a gun on it. On 23 January Commandant Hendrik Prinsloo of the Carolina Commando had on Burger's instructions climbed to the summit to inspect it. There he conferred with Commandant Salomon Grobler of the Vryheid Commando, who had been on the summit with the burghers for some time. They found a suitable position for a gun. Members of the German Corps were detailed to prepare a gunpit. They completed that task the same evening, during which an attempt was made to drag a gun to the summit. They were unsuccessful and the gun was taken down again.

On the night of 23 January there were approximately 195 Vryheid burghers and German Corps volunteers on the summit. The night

The spur up which Major-General Sir ERP Woodgate's force advanced on the night of 23 January.

was a quiet one along the Thukela line, with only a signal lamp flashing occasionally and an isolated shot disturbing the silence.

From 19:00 the British force began assembling in a small valley a few kilometres west of Spioenkop. It was a cool, overcast evening, which turned into a pitch dark night, with intermittent drizzle. Just prior to setting off, instructions were issued that there was to be no talking, smoking, lights taken along or firing without orders. Every effort was being made to surprise the Boers. The force set off shortly after 21:00. Lieutenant-Colonel Thorneycroft, followed immediately by his own men, led the way. Progress in the pitch dark was very slow. Periodically the column was halted while

Thorneycroft and a few others went ahead to seek out landmarks, before everyone advanced again. Thorneycroft had earlier taken careful prior note of the distinguishing features along the route and was able to lead the column without getting lost. The column's steady advance was punctuated by the constant clink of nails, rifles and equipment on the many stones along the route.

First they proceeded along a narrow valley, then across a broader one, until they reached the spur they were to climb to the summit. The route up the spur was stone strewn and consisted of a series of steep sections followed by little plateaus. The darkness made it more difficult to negotiate. Despite this the British column made steady and unhindered progress up the spur, with Thorneycroft locating one landmark after the other, until eventually he reached a sparse clump of trees on a small plateau near the summit.

It was now approximately 02:00 on 24 January. The men were formed into lines, bayonets were fixed and then everyone lay down in the wet grass, waiting for the troops at the back to catch up. Tension mounted as they waited in the pitch darkness. With everyone ready the advance recommenced, up the last steep slope and then on to the summit. They had not proceeded far on the summit before a loud challenge came, "Werda!" from one of 15 Vryheid burghers on picket duty. The British flung themselves to the ground. The burghers opened fire, but apart from two or three soldiers who were lightly wounded the rest escaped unscathed. As soon as the burghers' magazines were empty, Thorneycroft ordered a "Charge". The picket was routed, leaving one dead. All the Boers fled from the summit. It was now about 03:40.

Woodgate's force now gave three mighty cheers to signal their success to Warren. Star shells were then fired to signal the success

General Schalk Burger, responsible for the sector from Spioenkop to Brakfontein.

to the entire British line. After a hasty, but inadequate examination of the summit the Engineers indicated where a trench was to be dug. The trench, approximately 300 to 400 metres long faced generally northwards, with both extremities slightly drawn back and thus facing west and eastwards. Hard soil and solid rock made it impossible to dig a proper trench, especially as the heavier and more effective trenching tools had been left half way down the spur when they became too burdensome to carry. The resultant trench was shallow, offering adequate cover against rifle but not shell fire. By 06:30 the trench was completed. A thick mist still shrouded the summit. Critics maintain that parts of the trench were very poorly placed. From an examination of the battlefield it is difficult to imagine, given the shape of the hill, where else it could have been placed, without in one way or other exposing the men to serious dangers.

The initial firing on Spioenkop alerted the Boers in their encampments that all was not well, a situation soon confirmed by the burghers who fled from the summit and arrived in both Burger's and Botha's laagers to the east and north of Spioenkop respectively. Burger appears to have become panicky. Messages he despatched about the capture of Spioenkop during the course of the morning make it clear that he was very pessimistic. He ordered Hendrik Prinsloo to counter-attack by storming the hill with approximately 80 Carolina men. Prior to carrying out this instruction, Prinsloo ordered 30 of his men under Corporal Smit to climb Spioenkop in an effort to establish what the British were doing. After this Prinsloo made his way to Botha in order to inform him of events that had taken place on Spioenkop and make further plans to repulse the British.

Botha's reaction to the new threat was immediate and decisive. He ordered Prinsloo to storm the hill, up the steep grassy north-eastern slope, promising to send reinforcements as well as giving supporting rifle and shell fire from the north and north-west, while Burger was to provide supporting fire from the east. Prinsloo returned to Burger's laager, arriving there at approximately 06:00. Orders were given for a Krupp to be placed well up the slope of the western Twin Peak, while a Pom-Pom gun was brought into position on the ridge linking Aloe Knoll and the Twin Peaks. The Spioenkop summit was well within range of both guns.

Fifty burghers were ordered on to Aloe Knoll, which is attached to the summit and a mere 400 metres from the British trench. This strategic knoll was still completely hidden by the mist from the British, who were unaware of its significance. Its strategic value could only be appreciated from the Boer side. The Boers already on Green Hill were ordered to give supporting fire to the counter attack as soon as they could see something.

The four guns on iNtabamnyama – a 37mm Maxim-Nordenfeldt, a 75mm Krupp gun and two 75mm Creusot guns – were ordered to swing round and prepare to fire on to the summit when it became light. Two of these guns were brought closer to Spioenkop. There was

The Carolina Commando camp which was situated on the northern slope between the Twin Peaks.

also a 75mm Krupp to the north-east of Spioenkop, near Botha's headquarters. Additional men were ordered to leave their positions on iNtabamnyama and make their way towards the north-eastern slope of Spioenkop where they were to assist the Carolina commando with the counter attack.

The burghers who eventually advanced up the north-eastern slope numbered approximately 400 and were drawn from the Pretoria, Krugersdorp, Standerton, Johannesburg, Carolina commandos and the German Corps. Members of the Boksburg Commando occupied Conical Hill, situated at the end of a spur north of Spioenkop. The Boers were making full use of the cover provided by the darkness and mist to prepare systematically for a counter attack.

S mit's handful of men made contact with the British while it was still dark. After only a few shots were exchanged they retired partway down the steep north-eastern slope. At 07:15 Woodgate felt confident enough on the mist-shrouded summit to send the following message to Warren:

> "We have entrenched a position, and are, I hope secure; but the fog is too thick to see...".

However, when the mist partially lifted for a short while soon afterwards, he realised immediately that part of the trench was poorly placed. From near its centre (where the main British memorial now stands) to the right extremity, the downward slope of the ground from the trench towards the north-eastern crest, created dead ground, which would allow the Boers to crawl, undetected in places, to within 50 metres of his trench. The Engineers were quickly ordered forward on to the crest-line to establish another trench and remedy the situation. From this new position the British would be able to see the Boers trying to climb the steep slopes of Spioenkop.

As the sappers attempted to build the new defence line on the stony crest-line they were fired on. But soldiers who had come forward to support them, gave them covering fire. Soon the mist again completely enveloped the summit and brought an end to all firing. Under cover of this mist, elements of the Royal Lancasters, Thorneycroft's Mounted Infantry and Lancashire Fusiliers were ordered to move on to the crest-line from which presumably they would be able to see down all the steep slopes, up which the Boers were likely to advance. There is no record of precisely how many

Commandant Hendrik Prinsloo, the inspirational commander of the Carolina Commando.

men moved onto the crest-line. The line they held stretched approximately 350 to 400 metres. This movement from the trench to the crest-line must have taken place sometime between 07:30 and 08:00. The British now held two positions. The forward one along the crest and the second one in the trench over the highest part of the hill. As the ground was so hard and stony the Engineers were unable to construct a trench and the soldiers had to make do with what little natural cover there was on the crest-line.

In the meantime Prinsloo gathered most of the rest of his men and rode across to the mist-shrouded Spioenkop. There they unsaddled in the gully between Spioenkop and Aloe Knoll at the foot of the steep slope. Part of the way up Spioenkop he encountered Smit's men, who had been on the slope for some time and were able to hear the British soldiers working away at their trenches. Before continuing up the slope he is said to have addressed the burghers as follows,

"Burgers, ons gaan onder die vyand in en ons sal nie almal terugkom nie. Doen julle plig en vertrou op die Here." (Burghers, we are going in amongst the enemy and all of us will not return. Do your duty and have trust in the Lord.)

As the Boers reached or neared the crest-line they came under heavy fire. They were almost amongst the British soldiers holding the crest-line and suffered most heavily on their right flank (where the present-day road goes past the Boer memorial and also near where the memorial stands). Having been taken somewhat by surprise in the mist, many burghers fled down the slope. Prinsloo managed to halt them at a stone ledge where they took cover. From there they moved further to their left, where they noticed more cover. The early fighting was at very close quarters, with opponents at times lying on either side of the same boulder. Casualties were high.

At approximately 08:00 or soon after, the sun finally broke through the mist and transformed the odds on the battlefield. It was only now that Woodgate could see precisely the death trap he and his men were in. They did have possession of the highest part of the hill, but it was an open, bald summit, on which they were extremely exposed. The Boers were already lodged on the north-eastern slope, if somewhat precariously. But more seriously they occupied Aloe Knoll, from where they could look into part of the British trench and had an excellent view of those soldiers holding the right extremity on the crest-line. There were also the burghers on Conical Hill and Green Hill, who were able to direct a fire on some of the British soldiers who had advanced on to the northern and north-western crest-line.

As the mist cleared the burgher fire increased in intensity, lending support to Prinsloo's party who were holding on with some difficulty. Prinsloo signalled by heliograph to Botha, requesting reinforcements. Botha replied that he had already despatched 400 men. During the course of the morning these men joined the Carolina commando. The Boer gunners on iNtabamnyama and the Twin Peaks had a clear view of the soldiers on the summit and sent an ever-increasing barrage of shells which burst over or near the British positions. The Boer shell fire had a catastrophic effect on the

British soldiers during the course of the day. The early blanket of mist had created a false sense of security among Woodgate's men. Now they had to deal with reality.

Major-General Sir ERP Woodgate died of wounds received on Spioenkop. He was buried at St John's Church cemetery, Mooi River.

To add to the British adversity, at approximately 08:30 Woodgate was struck in the head and mortally wounded. This created tremendous confusion as to who was in command. Initially Lieutenant-Colonel Blomfield succeeded Woodgate, but he also was soon wounded and the command then devolved on Lieutenant-Colonel Crofton of the Royal Lancasters. Once Warren heard of Woodgate's loss he ordered Coke to climb the hill and assume the command. Coke commenced his ascent at 11:10. When Buller heard that Coke had assumed the command he suggested that a hard fighting man like Thorneycroft be put in command. Warren agreed to this and sent the following message to Crofton, "With the approval of the Commander-in-Chief, I place Lt-Col Thorneycroft in command of the summit..."; however, Warren failed to inform Coke of Thorneycroft's promotion. Coke did not become aware of this change in command and continued to make his way to the summit, albeit slowly, as he was still recovering from a fractured leg. It was only late in the afternoon, when he eventually climbed to the summit, having spent most of the day encamped part of the way up the spur, that he was informed that Thorneycroft had in fact been in command for several hours. It was from his position on the spur that Coke, with no clear picture of the conditions on the summit, in a rather indirect way proceeded to influence the battle. To add to the confusion Coke at one stage ordered Lieutenant-Colonel Hill, commander of the Middlesex Regiment who went up as reinforcements, to assume command on the summit.

This chaotic state was further compounded by poor communications existing between the battlefield and Warren, after the signal station on the summit was destroyed by a Boer shell. From then onwards messages sent to and from Warren had to be relayed via Buller on Mount Alice because it was too dangerous to take up a position from which to signal directly to Warren's camp.

The Boers gain the ascendancy

As the morning sun blazed down on the summit with increasing intensity, so the battle became more ferocious. Conditions for the British became critical, with rifle and artillery fire converging on them from an arc of 150 degrees. Eventually Crofton sent a message to Warren imploring him "Reinforce at once or all lost. General dead." This message, received at 09:50, made it clear that conditions were far more serious than Warren had previously been led to believe. Both Buller and Warren despatched reinforcements to the summit.

It was on the British right that the most intense fighting was taking place, with fire coming from Aloe Knoll, the Boers on the slope and in some cases already on the crest. In places the Lancashire Fusiliers had been driven off the crest back into the trench. To counteract this,

Lieutenant Grothaus, standing behind the tip of the gun, was a German national who served with the Boer artillery on iNtabamnyama.

Thorneycroft sent out a party of 20 men from the trench to drive the Boers away from their newly captured positions on the lip of the summit. A hail of fire brought this effort to a quick halt and considerable losses were suffered. Thorneycroft then personally gathered together 40 men and attempted to charge and drive the Boers down the slope. As the Boers became aware of this new threat they opened another deadly hail of fire on it and checked Thorneycroft's men long before they could reach the summit edge, inflicting heavy losses. Thorneycroft himself fell during this charge and twisted his knee. He managed however to crawl back to the trench, reaching it unwounded.

Many burghers were accompanied to the front by an African or "coloured" servant. These servants were known as "agterryers" (after riders) and formed an integral component of the Boer military system. There is an account of such a servant being killed on the Spioenkop summit.

If the British were suffering so were the Boers. Deneys Reitz of the Pretoria Commando described conditions as follows,

"The English troops lay so near that one could have tossed a biscuit among them, and whilst the losses which they were causing us were only too evident, we on our side did not know that we were inflicting even greater damage upon them. Our own casualties lay hideously among us ..."

The Boers who had taken firm control of the eastern-most end of the summit edge now slowly but systematically drove these British still on the crest-line back to the trench. By approximately 11:45 the Boers had captured the entire north-eastern part of the crest. There were still some British soldiers in forward positions along the north-western part of the crest-line. The Boers along the north-eastern crest-line now concentrated their fire on those soldiers in the trench from its centre to the right extremity. The Boer gunners also focused their attention on the trench from this stage onwards. The Boer artillery fire was guided by Louis Bothma, Prinsloo's signaller who was situated somewhere on the north-eastern summit edge from where he operated a heliograph and had an excellent view of where the shells were bursting. With his assistance the shell fire became murderously accurate, with the battle reaching a new intensity. One of Thorneycroft's men described the scene as follows,

"The most awful carnage. We had no guns... Shells rained in amongst us. The most hideous sights were exhibited. Men blown to atoms, joints torn asunder. Headless bodies, trunks of bodies. Awful. Awful. You dared not lift your head above the Rock or you were shot dead at once. Everything was confusion, officers were killed or mixed up in other regiments, the men had no one to rally them and became demoralised..."

The Boers lying along the north-eastern summit edge were eventually in a far better position than were the soldiers in the trench before them. Because of the slope and position of the trench on the top of the summit, the British soldiers' heads became outlined on the skyline. That is why the soldier quoted above mentions that "You dared not lift your head...". The British also had no artillery fire to assist them. The main part of the battle was being fought out of sight from where Warren's guns were situated. They were also very far away, in stark contrast to the well and far more

closely placed artillery of Botha, whose fire was still being guided by Prinsloo's signaller, Louis Bothma.

As the battle stretched into the early afternoon, morale among the British soldiers on the far right flank, where the heaviest losses were caused, began to flag. The intense heat of the day and thirst were also taking their toll. At approximately 13:00 one of the Lancashire Fusiliers there, could tolerate it no more and raised a white flag. The Boers ceased firing and rose up to claim their prisoners, but were then fired upon from somewhere further along the British trench. The Boers immediately returned the fire, only to be greeted by more white flags from the Fusiliers. A few Boers led by Jan Cilliers of the Pretoria commando, then stormed forward to the trench, wanting to know who was surrendering. Numerous Fusiliers capitulated.

Thorneycroft's attention was drawn to the crisis in his trench. Accompanied by some of his men he dashed to the Boers at the trench and shouted, "I'm the commandant here; take your men back to hell, sir! There's no surrender." However, most of the Fusiliers were so demoralised that they began moving towards the Boer positions and surrendered. Thorneycroft and the remaining

Fusiliers and some of his men were forced to flee to a clump of rocks nearer the centre of the summit to seek cover. Part of the trench was now in Boer hands! These Boers were able to open a dangerous flanking fire on the British in the trench further to their right. Fortunately for Thorneycroft, some of the 2nd Middlesex Regiment reinforcements came into view at this moment. He ordered them to charge the burghers at the trench, forcing the Boers to retire to the summit edge.

The British collapse on the right flank signalled to the Boers that the British resolve was melting away. They therefore increased their pressure on the centre of the trench held by Crofton's Royal Lancasters, by creeping ever closer. The Lancasters' resolve, too, suddenly gave way and they ran from the trench (13:45). Crofton rushed towards them to rally them and ordered a bugler to sound the advance. At this critical and chaotic moment more Middlesex reinforcements arrived and charged through the panic-stricken men to re-occupy the deserted trench and help avert a disaster. Thorneycroft took up a position a little back from the centre of the trench from which he now conducted the battle ordering forward reinforcements where they were required and also constantly encouraging his men. The Boers did not again attempt to charge the trench. They relied on artillery and longer range rifle fire to cause further casualties among the soldiers. This damaging rifle and artillery fire was kept up until darkness. Otherwise this part of the battle remained static from 15:00 onwards.

It was on the British right, at approximately 14:00, that the Boers next mounted a concerted effort to outflank Lieutenant-Colonel Hill, of the Middlesex Regiment and members of the Imperial Light Infantry. Hill had taken up a position among some rocks (behind where the present day Imperial Light Infantry memorial stands), beyond the right extremity of the trench. The British had no trench in this position, but simply used the natural cover. Hill was so

Lieutenant-General Sir Charles Warren

engrossed in trying to hold on to his position that he was unaware that Thorneycroft was fighting an almost equally desperate battle at the trench. The heavy and accurate Boer fire eventually forced Hill to retreat from his position which was then occupied by the burghers.

If these burghers could advance another few metres along the southern slope of the hill, they would be ideally placed to attack Thorneycroft's position from the rear. At this extremely critical moment (15:45) reinforcements of the 1st Scottish Rifles spotted these Boers and opened fire on them. On the southern part of the summit, among the rocks, a desperate and crucial skirmish ensued, fought at very close quarters, about which Thorneycroft, due to the fierceness of the battle in the trench, was not aware. Eventually the Scottish Rifles managed to drive the burghers out of the threatening position they held and were able to re-occupy the rocks Hill was forced to vacate. Some of the Scots followed the retiring Boers down the slope towards Aloe Knoll, but as soon as they left the cover of the rocks they came under fierce fire, which forced them to retreat back to the rocks but not before a number of them were wounded or killed. From 16:30 this part of the battle, too, became static. The Boers did not attempt another charge on any of the British positions.

The next drama unfolded itself on the Twin Peaks. Much earlier in the day there had been calls for assistance from Thorneycroft. In response Warren called on Major-General Lyttelton, who was under the command of Buller at or near Mount Alice to "give every assistance...". Lyttelton sent reinforcements to the summit in the form of the Scottish Rifles and Bethune's Mounted Infantry. He also despatched the 3rd King's Royal Rifles Corps (KRR) to assist, by assaulting the Boer positions on the Twin Peaks, and thereby hoped to distract the Boers or bring additional pressure to bear on them. Lyttelton did not give Lieutenant-Colonel Riddel, commander of the KRR, detailed orders, rather leaving him to use his own discretion.

The Boers in their lofty positions on the Twin Peaks had an unimpeded view of the KRR advancing across the flat, open valley of the Thukela and soon opened a long-range rifle fire on them. Other than causing them to deploy, this had little effect on the KRR, who eventually reached the foot of the steep hills. Once they were ascending the hills (approximately 15:00) the very steepness of the slope was to their advantage, for, in order for the burghers to see them, they had to expose themselves on the skyline. The KRR were skilfully deployed so that while some of them advanced, the others lay in the grass and gave them covering fire, thus making it extremely dangerous for the Boers to take steady aim at them. Once the forward section had advanced sufficiently they would wait for those who had given covering fire to advance beyond them while in turn covering them.

When Buller heard that Lyttelton had sent the KRR to the Twin Peaks, he immediately ordered that the troops should be recalled, as he believed that the attack was too difficult. Lyttelton eventually complied

with this giving the necessary orders to the KRR at 15:00, 15:30 and 16:50, but received no response until 17:00 when Riddell stated,

> "If I can recall the advanced sections I will do so, but it is difficult to communicate, and the hill is fearfully steep..."

It was at about this time that the KRR captured the Twin Peaks forcing Burger and his men to retire in great haste, taking with them their gun and Pom-Pom gun that had caused so much damage during the course of the day and it was only when they arrived in one of the Boer laagers near Ladysmith that he halted! The KRR had punched a considerable hole in the Boer defence line.

From the summit Riddell signalled his success back to camp, stating that he would remain there unless ordered to retire. The reply came almost immediately from Major Bayly, Lyttelton's staff officer, "Retire when dark." This is a somewhat surprising order considering the KRR were in an excellent position to threaten those Boers, especially on Aloe Knoll, who had made it so intolerable for Thorneycroft's right flank on the summit. Buller seems to have failed to grasp the significance of the success. He missed a golden opportunity to turn the tables on the Boers. Soon after Riddell reached the summit he was killed. As ordered, the KRR retired back to camp once it became dark.

The final phase, retreat and repercussions

It was sometime after 17:00 that Coke finally made his way on to the summit for the first time. The sight of the retreating wounded and demoralised troops, as well as accounts from various officers made him realise just how grave the situation was.

He therefore sent the following message to Warren,

"The original troops are still in position, have suffered severely, and the dead and wounded are still in the trenches. The shell-fire is, and has been severe. If I hold on to the position all night, is there any guarantee that our artillery can silence the guns? Otherwise to-day's experience will be repeated, and the men will not stand another complete day's shelling...The situation is extremely critical...should you wish me to retire, cover retirement..."

This message unfortunately only reached Warren at 20:00. Until that time he was still under the impression that conditions were difficult, but not critical. He had however not made every effort to acquaint himself with conditions on the summit. Furthermore he had not kept Thorneycroft informed that efforts were being made to bring artillery on to the summit and that supplies were also being sent. Soon after the arrival of Coke's message Winston Churchill, who had been on the summit earlier during the day, reported to Warren that conditions were extremely serious on the summit.

There was clearly a need for quick action now. In the dark Churchill was ordered back to the summit to inform Thorneycroft of all the preparations being made. A half hour later Colonel Sim of the Royal Engineers was also despatched to the summit where he was to construct emplacements for two naval guns and the mountain battery and to improve the trenches. He was to order Thorneycroft to hold the hill at all costs. The length, steepness and difficulty of terrain would have made it impossible to get naval guns on to the summit by dawn and the mountain guns were outranged by the Boer artillery and would therefore have been ineffective.

Bringing in the wounded from Spioenkop while the battle still raged. Reinforcements making their way to the summit complained that their advance was hindered by the wounded being brought down and soldiers who were leaving the battlefield.

All this was too late. Thorneycroft, who had all day been in or near the firing line, was exhausted by now. As the sun began to set the Boer rifle and artillery fire picked up in intensity yet again, causing him to wonder whether the men would be able to hold on much longer. In a message to Warren he stated,

> "...I consider that even with reinforcements which have arrived, it is impossible to permanently hold this place so long as the enemy's guns can play on the hill...The enemy are now (6.30) firing from both flanks (rifle, shell, and Nordenfeldt), while a heavy rifle-fire is being kept up on the front. It is all I can do to hold my own... The situation is critical."

While Warren was finally receiving information which made him realise that circumstances on the summit were critical, Thorneycroft was convening a council-of-war with Lieutenant-Colonel Cooke, of the Scottish Rifles, and Crofton, to discuss whether they should remain on the summit or retire. Other than being informed that he was in command and the reinforcements that were sent to the summit, Thorneycroft had received little material assistance from Warren. The Boer artillery fire, which was the greatest problem, had continued unabated. It is likely that Thorneycroft felt himself deserted by now and therefore decided to take his own decision regarding further action. Thorneycroft's attitude was, "Better six battalions safely off the hill than a mop-up in the morning". The others soon agreed and by 20:15 the retirement began. Soon after the troops began to retire, Hill became aware of his own Middlesex Regiment withdrawing. Believing himself to be in command, he halted them and in the dark went in search of Thorneycroft. When he finally found him, there was a dispute as to who was in command. Only now did it become clear to Hill that he was not in command. With that the withdrawal continued. Hill and Thorneycroft had therefore been on the summit for over six hours both believing they were in command.

When Churchill located the mentally and physically exhausted Thorneycroft on the summit, he gave him Warren's note. But Thorneycroft's mind was made up and he continued with the withdrawal. Thorneycroft gave the following message to Churchill for Warren,

> "Regret to report that I have been obliged to abandon Spion Kop, as the position became untenable..."

At about midnight Thorneycroft encountered Sim and his party at the bottom of the spur. Sim showed him the letter from Warren. Thorneycroft stated that it was too late to return and ordered Sim to withdraw his work party. Captain Phillips acting on behalf of Coke also tried to halt the retreat, but to no avail. Those who had spent so many hours on the summit were in no mood to remain there and probably were also aware of the futility.

It was only some time after 02:00 that an exhausted Thorneycroft stumbled into Warren's tent to report that he had led the force off the summit. This was the first Warren heard that a retirement had taken place. He promptly informed Buller. Buller had already set off for Warren's camp and met the messenger soon after 05:00. Buller arrived in Warren's camp at 06:00 and immediately assumed full command and announced that all the men who had been under Warren's control were to withdraw across the river. Buller gave four reasons for this decision.

British dead ready for burial on 26 January 1900 in a trench the Boers had probably dug on Spioenkop prior to the battle. The army chaplain reported burying 243 British soldiers on the summit over three days. Fifteen Boers also lie buried on the summit.

These were: the force had been in continuous action for a week; there had been heavy losses on Spioenkop; Warren had mixed up the brigades, and lastly, the positions they held were dangerously insecure.

Meanwhile the onset of darkness had resulted in many burghers on the summit being seized by uncertainty and fear. Just like the British they were also exhausted, thirsty and tired; and their dead were covered with swarms of flies attracted by the smell of blood. To add to their difficulties they were feeling insecure on the summit as the British had seized the Twin Peaks. They were unaware that that position and Spioenkop were being evacuated. In these circumstances the majority of burghers also began to retreat from Spioenkop, eventually reducing the number of men on the summit to approximately 60 to 80 burghers. Not even the fierce Commandant Opperman of the Pretoria Commando, was able to check the withdrawal.

Botha was convinced that the British would retreat. They had been ineffective on iNtabamnyama, suffered considerably on Spioenkop and had not followed up their success on the Twin Peaks; however, in the event of his having misjudged the situation he gave instructions for 250 Heidelbergers, 50 Krugersdorpers and 30 Pretorians to gather at the foot of Spioenkop in readiness to resume the struggle on the 25th.

Conclusions

I n the early hours of 25 January Lieutenant (Doctor) Blake Knox and a party of ambulance men made their way to the summit to attend to the wounded and dead. A horrific sight greeted them on the battlefield. It was strewn with wounded and dead.

Many of the dead were horribly mutilated. They had not been working for long, when they were suddenly challenged by Boers who surrounded them. Because they were not wearing the necessary Red Cross insignia they were taken prisoner. When Botha arrived on the summit and Knox was able to convince him of his bona fides he was released to continue with his task, but not before being given a cigarette and coffee. Many of the burghers on the summit picked whatever useful items they could find on the battlefield.

They also cut off buttons from the corpses' uniforms. Burying the dead in the hard soil was an extremely arduous task. The British consequently buried many of their dead in the shallow trenches. The burial of 243 British dead on the summit took three days. The Boers removed most of their dead from the summit. Fifteen burghers were buried on the summit.

While the burial was proceeding on the summit, the British force began retiring across the Thukela River at Trichardt's Drift. By the afternoon of 27 January the entire force was back in camp without the Boers having made any effort to attack while they were vulnerable. Botha argued that his men were exhausted after all the fighting and were therefore in no condition to launch a counter-attack. An opportunity had none the less been lost.

Sorting the dead from the wounded. When the war began approximately 1 000 Indians offered their services as unpaid ambulance assistants. The Indian Ambulance Corps played a significant role in assisting the wounded at Spioenkop.

Casualties

There is no agreement on the exact losses suffered during the battle. Approximate casualties were:

Boer		British	
Killed	58	Killed	322
Wounded	140	Wounded	563
		Missing/Prisoners	300

Comments

Buller, in a secret report to the Secretary of State for War, made it quite clear that Warren was to blame for the disaster. It appears that the man who already carried the blame for the Colenso debacle wanted to distance himself as far as possible from this fiasco. However, as mentioned earlier, why was he, the commander and man with more experience, not in command of the larger force, confronted with the far more difficult task? Was he trying to ensure that any further reverse would not be his immediate responsibility? And, if Warren were successful, then he would be able to take the credit for having initiated the movement.

There were other tactical errors made during the campaign on the upper Thukela. The British officers generally employed only a small portion of their force against a numerically inferior enemy. If Clery had made a concerted attack on the Boers before him on iNtabamnyama on 24 January they would have been extremely hard pressed, especially when one considers how successful Lyttelton was with one battalion at the Twin Peaks. Warren was also very slow in moving and failed to take advantage of unexpected success, such as that achieved by Dundonald.

Having withdrawn from the Spioenkop area Buller was no nearer to relieving Ladysmith than he was more than a month previously. The Boer defence line on the northern side of the Thukela was still intact. Less than two weeks later Buller made his next attempt to relieve Ladysmith, at Vaalkrans.

Units involved in the Spioenkop battle

Boer:

Commanding Officer: General Louis Botha

Carolina Commando	Ermelo Commando
German Corps	Johannesburg Commando
Heidelberg Commando	Standerton Commando
Krugersdorp Commando	Utrecht Commando
Pretoria Commando	Boksburg Commando
Rustenberg Commando	Lydenburg Commando
Vryheid Commando	Staatsartillerie

British:

Commanding Officer: Lieutenant-General Sir Charles Warren

Naval guns	17th Royal Engineers
Imperial Light Infantry	2nd Royal Lancaster Regiment
3rd King's Royal Rifles Corps	1st Scottish Rifles Regiment
2nd Lancashire Fusiliers	1st South Lancashire Regiment
2nd Middlesex Regiment	Thorneycroft's Mounted Infantry

Bringing in the wounded from Spioenkop.

Feb. 3rd 1900

My dear Jim

I can only write hurriedly as I am busy night and day reorganizing my Regt. Our loss was terribly severe. I led them up the hill 180 strong and we came back 90 – 7 officers and 21 men killed 4 officers and 43 men wounded 16 men missing (almost certain to have been killed and no card of identification on them) 2 since dead of wounds. I am now 17 officers short, killed wounded and sick which makes it difficult to carry on.

I enclose a copy of telegram which Buller sent home about me. I did order the retirement as the place was untenable for another day unless the Boers' artillery could be kept down and we had no position in our possession from which this could be done. The attack on Spion Kop <u>should have been</u> part of a general plan of attack and directly it was known that we had carried the crest at 4 a.m. (and it was known at once) the hill to N.E. of our position should have been carried at the point of bayonet. We should then have been able to bring our artillery to bear on the Boer guns. As it was the Boer artillery were invisible to all except us on the hill and no artillery could have come into action on the top under the <u>close rifle fire</u> of the enemy – and the naval guns which it was afterwards suggested should have come up could not have been dragged up the rocks till a proper road had been prepared. I want you to understand the case as it is bound to be the cause of criticism. <u>Buller's opinion is good enough for me</u>. We had no water for 24 hours. The wounded got a little sent up by Warren. The Boers had 2 Maxim Nordenfel(d)t 1 1/4 lb shell guns. They fire 1 to 20 shots one after another and the little shells come buzzing round. The moral effect is good. ... The Boers fired our own shrapnel taken at Colenso at Spion Kop.

Copy of Sir Redvers Buller's despatch cable 31.1.1900

Colonel Thorneycroft was the officer who ordered the retirement from Spion Kop. ... I believe his personal gallantry saved a difficult situation early in the day on the 24th and that with a loss of at least 40 percent he conducted the defence with conspicuous courage and ability throughout the day – no blame whatever, for the withdrawal is, in my opinion attributable to him and I think his conduct throughout was admirable.

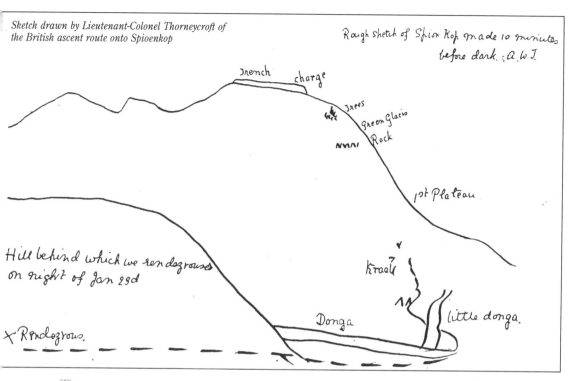

Sketch drawn by Lieutenant-Colonel Thorneycroft of the British ascent route onto Spioenkop

Rough sketch of Spion Kop made 10 minutes before dark. : A. W. J.

Trench   charge

Trees

Green Glacis

Rock

1st Plateau

Hill behind which we rendezvoused on night of Jan 23d

kraal

× Rendezvous.

Donga

little donga.

Battlefield - General information

The entrance gate to the battlefield opens at sunrise and closes at sunset.

Be prepared to spend at least an hour at the battlefield. A self-guided trail, beginning and ending at the car park, has been established on the summit of the hill. A pamphlet guide is available which explains the key events of the battle at strategically selected, marked spots along the trail. The battlefield is well preserved.

Additional Reading

Amery, L.S. *The Times History of the War in South Africa* Vol III (London, Sampson Low, Marston and Company, 1905).

Barnard, C.J. *Generaal Louis Botha op die Natalse Front, 1899 - 1900* (Cape Town, AA Balkema, 1970).

Breytenbach, J.H. *Die Geskiedenis van die Tweede Vryheidsoorlog in Suid Afrika* Vol III (Pretoria, Die Staatsdrukker, 1969-1978).

Pakenham, Thomas. *The Boer War* (Johannesburg, Jonathan Ball, 1979).

Reitz, D. *Commando* (Johannesburg, Jonathan Ball, 1983).

Symons, J. *Buller's Campaign* (London, The Cresset Press, 1963).

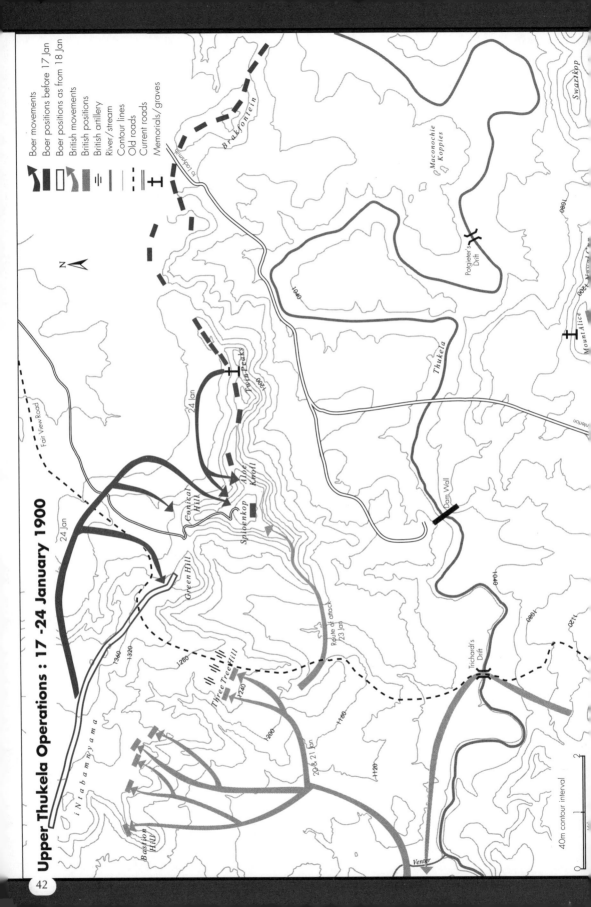

Upper Thukela Operations : 17 -24 January 1900

Boer movements
Boer positions before 17 Jan
Boer positions as from 18 Jan
British movements
British positions
British artillery
River / stream
Contour lines
Old roads
Current roads
Memorials / graves

N

iNtabamnyama

Bastion Hill

Venter

1360
1320
1280
Three Tree Hill
1200
1200
1180
1160
1120

20 & 21 Jan

24 Jan

Fair View Road

Green Hill

Conical Hill
Spioenkop
Aloe Knoll
Twin Peaks
1200

24 Jan

to Ladysmith

Brakfontein

Route of attack 23 Jan

Trichardt's Drift
1040
1080
1120

Dam Wall

Thukela

1040

1040

Maconochie Koppies

Potgieter's Drift

Mount Alice

Swartkop

Merton

40m contour interval

42

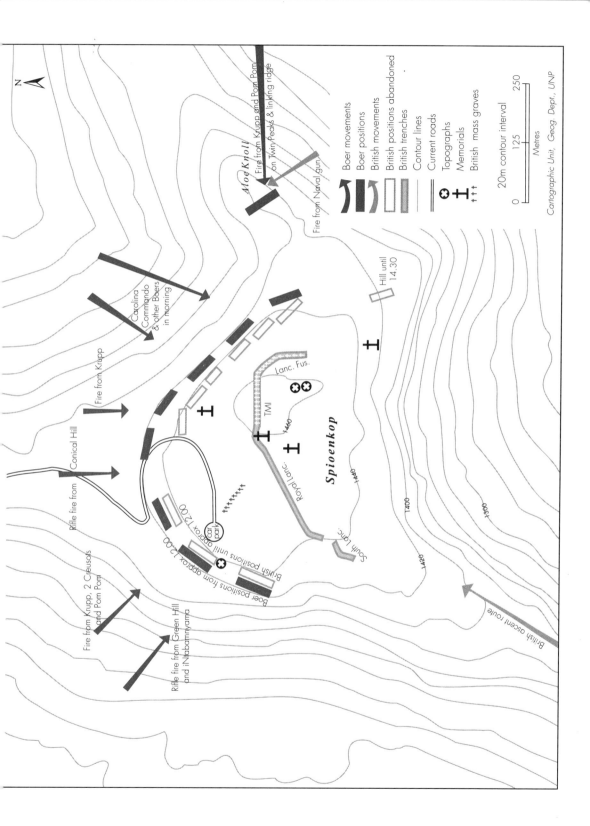

N

Aloe Knoll

Fire from Krupp and Pom Pom
on Twin Peaks & linking ridge

Fire from Naval gun

Boer movements
Boer positions
British movements
British positions abandoned
British trenches
Contour lines
Current roads
Topographs
Memorials
British mass graves

20m contour interval

Metres
0   125   250

Cartographic Unit, Geog. Dept., UNP

Carolina
Commando
& other Boers
in morning

Fire from Krupp

Rifle fire from Conical Hill

Fire from Krupp, 2 Creusots
and Pom Pom

Rifle fire from Green Hill
and iNtabamnyama

British positions until approx 12.00

Boer positions from approx 12.00

Hill until
14.30

Lanc. Fus.

TMI

Royal Lanc.

Spioenkop

South Lanc.

1460

1440

1400

1420

1300

British ascent route

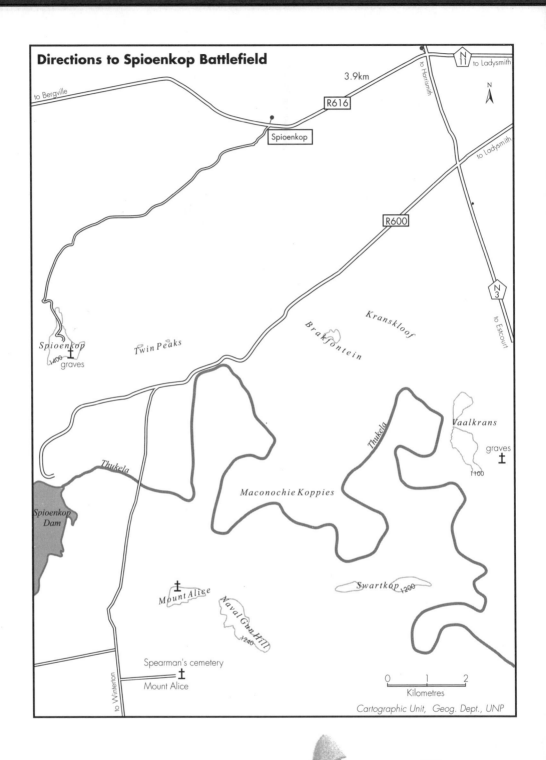

Directions to Spioenkop Battlefield

to Ladysmith

3.9km

to Harrismith

N
11

to Bergville

R616

Spioenkop

N

to Ladysmith

R600

N
3

to Estcourt

Kranskloof

Brakfontein

Spioenkop
1400
graves

Twin Peaks

Thukela

Vaalkrans

graves
1100

Maconochie Koppies

Thukela

Spioenkop
Dam

Swartkop 1200

Mount Alice

Naval Gun Hill
1240

Spearman's cemetery

Mount Alice

to Winterton

0   1   2
Kilometres

Cartographic Unit, Geog. Dept., UNP